GOD'S DAUGHTER

THE PRAYER WARRIOR

TAMERIA WEAVER

ISBN: 978-1-7378814-0-7

Any references to historical events, real people, or real places are
used fictitiously. Names, characters, and places are products of the
author's imagination.

Book design by Hoveify
Academy of Visions Publishing

Printed by Amazon KDP, Inc., in the United States of America.
First printing edition 2021.

womeninspiringnetwork.com

FOREWORD

It's an honor, and I am thankful for the opportunity to write the foreword for this book, God's Daughter The Prayer Warrior, written by my spiritual daughter, Elder Tameria Weaver. The first time I heard this woman of God speak, one word came to my mind, POWERFUL! She was excited about God and His power moving through her. I remember saying to myself; God is going to use her one day. I knew she was sincere, and she was not ashamed to let everybody know. As I have gotten to know her, I see her passion for women, which translates beyond just someone saying they love it. She shows her love for the women through her service. Building women has become critical because she knows what it is to be broken. It takes pain to produce the power that I see in Tameria, and in this book, she is transparent about her pain and struggles. Reading God's daughter will encourage women to understand what it means to be the daughter of the True and Living King.

Readers will realize they have the power to become all that God created them to be. Tameria has become that prayer warrior that she encourages others to become. I genuinely hope and believe that everyone who reads this book will shift and reach beyond the boundaries that have been set before them and be all God wants them to be.
Elder Tameria has decided to stand up and boldly navigate through life as God's daughter, and so should you.
Rise God's daughter and become that prayer warrior for the Kingdom! Activate your faith and move forward towards your purpose!

Daughter, you have made me proud, and I pray that every person that reads this book will be blessed by the insight God has given you to write it. Your Pastor! **–Dier Hopkins**

CONTENTS

Foreword
Letter from the Author
Acknowledgments
Letter From The Author

ACKNOWLEDGMENTS

No matter what road you take and what journey you began, I have realized that you need a team of people to assist you with the vision and push the purpose. Throughout my life, I've been blessed with people that have come into my space that genuinely want to see me birth what God has placed inside of me. I am grateful to the many men and women that have influenced my walk and have encouraged me not to give up. Without these people, I would have never been able to board this flight and to be able to take off.

Jamaal Weaver, my husband, thank you for remaining in my corner and seeing about our family. I know there were times he prayed to God on my behalf. I am grateful for my three young kings, who have been supportive and have been watching. Joseph, Christian, and Chase, I thank God for choosing me to be your mother. Being your mother has taught me to live beyond myself and see what value I bring to the lives of those watching. I pray daily to be a good example.

To my mother, who has always been my number #1 cheerleader. Thank you for always believing in the vision God gives and finding ways to ensure the vision is birthed. My sister who rides with me where ever. Chelsea, thank you, sis, for being you and always being there for my boys and me. My father for coming and speaking life. Thank you for mending and putting together things I didn't know were broken. My spiritual mother, for praying and seeing me through and holding me accountable for areas weakened but fasting until I reach strength. My bestie for making me feel like no goal I've set or the one God has set for me is unreachable. Thank you for making sure I stay believing in myself.

To my New Direction Church Family, thank you from the bottom of my heart. I thank God for my leaders, Pastor Dier Hopkins & First Lady Carrie Hopkins thank you for being great examples in my life. I thank God you have been patient with me through my brokenness and have pushed me to continue to be the best version of myself. Most of all, thank you for not allowing me to give up because you saw more. I thank God for the leadership team of ministers and elders who have constantly sent me reminders of who God is. Thank you for your encouraging words on the prayer line every morning, some of which I was able to grab and use as nuggets in this book. Thank you for accepting me on the team and believing in me. I pray that God continues to blow your minds and expand you for his glory and his kingdom. Thank you to the Women Inspiring & Networking ladies, my sisters, mothers, aunts, and cousins. You ladies have always believed in me, even when I didn't believe myself. God truly has shown me that fruit has come from this group. To see so many of you grow and blossom in your own relationships with God has truly been my place of rejoicing. Ladies, you have been a witness to so many trials and tribulations; you've reminded me that you stand right behind me. Thank you.

Hey sis!

I want you to have a seat, get comfortable and open your heart as you read this letter. You do such a great job of holding everything together, but I know that it's not always easy. In some areas, you are uncertain about your life plans and God's plan for your life. Sometimes you worry about your future. You spend time wondering if you will ever achieve the level of greatness that you so desperately desire. I know you have stood back and watched others receive some of the same things you've been praying for. It looks as if it's everyone else's turn, and you are still waiting and trusting God for your moment.

As you continue to go through life, there will be seasons when things seem impossible. Don't let those moments discourage you. There is always a goal to tackle, a task to complete, and moment to conquer, a quest to journey, a prayer that is waiting to manifest, a relationship needing mending, someone waiting for your forgiveness to start over, or even an opportunity to not be so hard on yourself. I know because there are several things that I need to check off on my list as of today.

I'm learning that the process will not be perfect, and I will have moments of pain and disappointment. However, I am still a fighter, and I believe that God fights battles on my behalf daily.

I constantly strive to meet God where he is to make sure I stay the course. Do I get frustrated?

Absolutely! Have I ever felt fear overtaking faith at times?

Sure have, almost in any season where I've had to rely on God completely because my request was bigger than my resources.

Were there times where I have fallen? Whew... yes, so hard that I thought I would never get back up. When I went through my first divorce, I lost everything. I was trying to find happiness outside of myself and God. I lost my job, my car, my apartment; I felt as though I had nothing left. As I began to release myself from that prison of hurt and disbelief, God began to restore me. I had to rebuild my life all over again.

Sis, I'm sharing my story with you because I want you to know that where you are today isn't the whole story. There is so much more that God has in store for you. No matter how dark things are in your life at this present moment, remember, you are God's daughter, and he will take care of you always. Being a daughter of God has so many rewards. There are trials and tribulations that you are facing.

However, the bible gives us the blueprint for how to handle these difficult moments.

"My brethren, count it all joy when ye fall into divers' temptations, knowing this, that the trying of your faith worketh patience. But let patience have her perfect work, that ye may be perfect and entire, wanting nothing. If any of you lack wisdom, let him ask of God, that giveth to all men liberally, and upbraideth not; and it shall be given him." -James 1:2-5.

Trust God!! Sis, this is just a moment in your story; it won't last forever. I believe that the spirit of God will come into your heart while reading this book and send a fresh wind to shift you into your next dimension.

Sis, you're going to get through this season.

I love you,

Tameria Weaver

INTRODUCTION

As women, we wear so many hats and satisfy so many roles.

We are the heartbeat of our families, the glue that holds

everything together even when we are falling apart. We make

room for things when our plates are filled. While I take great

pride in being a woman and all the titles that come along with

it, I must admit that there were times when I have been

weighed down. All of the expectations of me began taking a

significant toll on me. The overwhelming feelings of anxiety

made it difficult to carry the load. I started to entertain

negative thoughts that made me believe that I wasn't enough.
Have you ever felt like you weren't enough? If you have, then
you know that the thoughts of self-doubt are very destructive
to your confidence.

The image of a woman is often associated with perfection.
When we fail to fit into the status quo of perfection, then
society deems us as not being enough. We then internalize
those feelings, and it leads to insecurities. Not just the
insecurity of self-image, but we become insecure with our
God-given gifts and abilities. Also, if we're not careful, we
forfeit God's will for our lives. When we lack confidence in
our God-given gifts, we began to build walls that separate us
from our purpose. This often leads to us becoming a prisoner
of our thoughts and prisoners of the opinions of others. And
before we know it, we're stuck, and we no longer view
ourselves from God's perspective. We start looking for
acceptance and validation from people, and we devalue the
approval and assurance that comes from God.

I've spent years feeling stuck and feeling inadequate. Although I knew what I was supposed to be doing, I struggled with operating in God's will for my life. I found myself seeking a co-signer for what God had spoken over my life. This led me down the path of self-doubt and fear. The things that once came easy for me felt like a daunting task. I was afraid to own my gifts, and I found myself stuck in a pit of despair. I began to shrink; I started to hold back and disengage. I was no longer living up to my full potential. I became a prisoner of self-doubt and fear. The quality of my life and relationships began to suffer. I desperately wanted to be free. I began to seek God and develop a relationship with him. During my intimate moments with God, he reminded me of who He created me to be. He reminded me that I am his daughter and that he has great plans for my life. Through prayer, he set me free, and he has given me the power to walk boldly in my purpose. I can now say with pure confidence that I am God's Daughter: The Prayer Warrior.

1 SELF-WORTH

For so many years, it was my desire to walk in complete freedom. I finally reached a place of pure exhaustion, and I knew that something had to change. I could no longer live in the confinement of fear and self-doubt. I became exhausted, and I desperately needed God to take control of my life. However, once I finally reached this point, my prayer life was suffering tremendously. There were times when I would go days without praying. I didn't consult God for anything. I allowed myself to believe that I could do it all on my own.

Here I was with my superwoman cape on looking crazy. I was convinced that I could handle whatever was thrown my way without giving anything to God. I have been known to put so many things on my plate. There are times when I want to say no, but I always find myself pulling out my superwoman cape, trying to save the day. I have moments where I really want to sit down and rest. There have been things that I have abandoned that I needed to get done just so I could help someone else. I remember there were times I would wake up to get my day started, and during that day, I was so exhausted from the activities from the night or weekend before. I would sit on the corner of my bed for hours, not wanting to move. I would sit and think of things I could eliminate or tasks that I was able to quit to have some sort of relief. At the start of each day, I knew the day meant getting my three boys ready for school, making sure they were fed, and making it to work on time. I would get to work and write out all that needed to be done that day and try to sort through what was important and what could wait. I was so burnt out.

The more I tried to fix things without God, the more distraught I became. Let me just be honest; my life was a mess. I knew how to look like I had it all together on the outside, but on the inside, I was a flat-out mess. You're probably wondering why I was trying to do everything and fix things on my own? Well, the truth is I felt unworthy. I somehow allowed my feelings of not being enough to spill over into my relationship with God. I would tell myself that God doesn't have time for little ol' me. I allowed myself to believe that I was insignificant to the one that created me. Let me just be honest; I was in bad shape. The treatment that I experienced from others became my expectation of the way I thought God would treat me. I found myself teaching and preaching about the goodness of God, but I was withholding myself from enjoying the true essence of who God is. I would encourage others to "cast their cares on Jesus because he loves them and cares for them." However, I had somehow convinced myself that the scripture didn't apply to me. I was preaching and teaching about how we are nothing without God, and I wasn't even talking to Him. The enemy had my mind, and I let him make me feel unworthy. All of the things that I had done and been through in my life made me feel that I didn't deserve to have an intimate relationship with God. Have you ever been so low that you didn't even feel worthy of prayers? If so, I'm here to tell you that there is nothing that you can do that will pull you away from the love and grace of our God. You are his daughter, and no matter how far away you feel from him, he is always right there. It is up to us to communicate with God and really get to know him.

Although I felt unworthy, I felt something pulling on my heart to just talk to God despite my feelings. The more I talked to him, the closer I felt to him. I realized that he had never left my side, and I have always been his daughter. Prayer has been my way of understanding who God is and what he wants for my life. I find myself consulting with God about everything now. *"In all thy ways acknowledge Him, and He will direct thy path"* –Proverbs 3:6

Once I finally developed a relationship with God, the walls that have kept me in bondage began to fall. I began talking to him about my purpose and my passions. In return, he began to reveal his promises to me. I now am able to walk freely, knowing that God is in control. I have taken off my superwoman cape because I no longer need it. *"His word is a lamp unto my feet, and a light unto my path"* –Psalm 119:105. Every day that I wake up is a reminder that God has more in store for me. I find myself striving daily to live in accordance with His will for my life. God has placed me in a position where he allows me to speak to his people and live to see the manifestation of prayers and conversations. I am honored to be his daughter.

Being the daughter of God is such a reward, but it also comes with great responsibility. As I began to accept the responsibility of being God's daughter, I found myself struggling to be perfect. I wanted to make all the right decisions. I didn't want anyone to see my battle scars. I became ashamed of what I had been through. At the time, I didn't know that God could use the ugliest situations in my life and make them beautiful. I want to take a moment to talk to the woman who is ashamed, the woman who is constantly hiding the pain of your past; you don't have to do that anymore. God wants to use every part of his story for his glory. You are his daughter; he loves every part of you. You don't have to dress up your past or accessorize your pain. He can, and he will use even the broken parts of you. Do you remember the bible story about the little boy who had two pieces of fish and five barley loaves? (See John 6:9) God used the little boy's lunch to feed 5,000. However, before he used it, he "broke it," and he "blessed it." I want to encourage you that God will bless what is broken in you, and he will use your story to spiritually feed thousands. Brokenness leads to

blessings. The way you have fixed yourself up for everyone

else is not the way you need to fix yourself up for God. You

don't have to be ashamed, and you don't have to be perfect.

SCRIPTURES

1. For we are God's masterpiece. He has created us anew in Christ Jesus, so we can do the good things he planned for us long ago. (Ephesians 2:10)

2. I praise you because I am fearfully and wonderfully made; your works are wonderful, I know that full well. (Psalm 46:5)

3. Your beauty should not come from outward adornment, such as elaborate hairstyles and the wearing of gold jewelry or fine cloths. Rather, it should be that of your inner self, the unfading beauty of a gentle and quiet spirit, which is of great worth in God's sight. (1 Peter 3:3-4)

4. She is more precious than rubies; nothing you desire can compare with her. Long life is her right hand; in her left hand are riches and honor. Her ways are pleasant ways, and al her paths are peace. She is a tree of life to those who take hold of her; those who hold her fast will be blesse. (Proverbs 3:15-18)

PRAYER FOR SELF-WORTH

Dear God,

Thank you for loving me unconditionally. Thank you for loving me despite my imperfections. Thank you for loving me at my best and also loving me at my worst. Thank you for choosing me to be your daughter.

I come to you with an open heart asking that you will fill me with your love. I ask that you will allow me to see myself the way that you see me. Allow me to see my beauty, my worth, and my purpose. I ask that my internal beauty shine outwardly. I ask that you increase my confidence so that I may boldly declare that I am your daughter.

God, I ask that you will give me confidence in the areas where I struggle with insecurities. Please remind me of my self-worth and help me to always know that I am your daughter.

Have your way in my life.

In Jesus Name.

Amen.

2 HEALING

Letting go of my need to be perfect has been one of the most challenging things to accept throughout my journey. I had no clue how much the fear of rejection has controlled me throughout my life. For so many years, I was overly concerned with being accepted by people. It caused me to strive for unrealistic perfection. I didn't know how damaging my need for perfection was at the time.

Over the years, dark, painful moments that I went through

took a toll on me. I was busy trying to heal everyone else, but I didn't give myself the same attention. On my job, I work to help patients recover from physical ailments. In my ministry, I help individuals heal from spiritual wounds.

Working as a medical assistant is rewarding because I see patients heal over a period of time. I'm always grateful to see the progression of each patient that comes to the clinic. On the days when I'm tired and don't have much strength, I'm encouraged by the patients' journey—the moment that you can aid in someone else's healing, it serves as a reminder of purpose. With every patient that I worked with, God began to groom me for an even greater purpose. He started to show me the parallels of physical and spiritual healing. When people come into a doctor's office, the idea is to get a checkup to ensure all things are well and still functioning. Some come to the doctor to replenish medication that has run low. Others come to the doctor because they are experiencing pain in their bodies, and they need to be nourished back to good health.

From a spiritual place, we may find ourselves in the same space. We come into the kingdom of God, and we seek God to ensure that we are still doing his will, functioning according to his will and purpose. Some of us come to the kingdom of God because we need to be replenished of what we have poured out to the world. Some come into God's Kingdom with battle scars, wounds, and pain from ministry, people, and family, just needing God to pour and heal us from the stem of hurt. Do you see the parallels? When we are not physically or spiritually well, we must find a place to be helped. What if I told you that God has the healing that you need?

God is Jehovah Rapha, means the Lord your healer (Exodus 15:26.) There is no pain that is too great for God to heal. When Jesus died on the cross, he did it with you in mind. His blood provides healing and wholeness. Knowing that you are God's daughter should let you know that you have access to healing powers. If you need emotional healing,

God has the ability to heal your deepest wounds. If you are having an issue in your relationship, God can heal the hearts of everyone involved. If you're having problems in your marriage, God has the power to reconcile differences. If you are struggling with addiction, God has the power to break every stronghold. If you are having a hard time dealing with grief, God can send peace that surpasses all understanding. If you are dealing with wounds from your childhood, God can wrap you in his love, renew your heart, and relieve the pain.

Can I make it a little personal? Some of us are needing healing from ourselves? I can envision your left eyebrow-raising right now. Uh oh, I struck a nerve. I can recall when I was walking around, not feeling like I wasn't good enough to operate in ministry. No matter how many times God would reveal what he has placed inside me, I still felt like I was missing something. I would pray for the house, car, and husband. After God has blessed my prayer and allowed it to manifest, I would turn around and ask God, "Well, what about my job?" I never felt fulfilled. Although God was doing what I asked of him, I somehow managed to suck the joy out of every blessing. I was so focused on what I lacked that I struggled to see all that I had. Who am I speaking to? Have you been blessed by God, and instead of taking a moment to bask in the manifestation of your blessing you move on to the next thing? We are sometimes so unsettled because we are always searching for the door marked "more." Can you praise God in the hallway while waiting on the keys to unlock your next blessing? Can you praise God in the room where the blessing was just released?

Stressing about what is coming next is a trauma response. Learning how to be grateful for what God has done and where you currently are is a sign of healing. There is a process that we must all go through. The patients who come in for an office visit may have to return for several more visits before they are completely healed. Remember, slight relief from the pain is a step in the right direction. For some patients, it's days, others weeks, some months, and even years. However, they keep coming to the doctor because they know that working with the doctor will help them get better. The same must apply to spiritual healing. Sometimes the pain lingers for longer than you would like, but you must continue to trust God and trust the process for complete recovery. Your process doesn't have to be perfect for you to receive healing. You are God's daughter, and you can ask him and believe him for whatever you need.

FROM HEALING TO WHOLENESS

When we open our hearts and allow God to heal us, we can experience what is to be whole. Wholeness is completeness in your spirit, soul, and body. You are filled with the fruits of the spirit (joy, peace, long-suffering, goodness, and faith), financial sufficiency, prosperity, peace from war, victory in every area. You will experience; Unity and oneness with the Father, Son, and Holy Spirit. "I will put My Spirit within you, and you will come to life, and I will place you on your own land. Then you will know that I, the Lord have spoken and done it, declares the LORD." –Ezekiel 37:14

SCRIPTURES

1. And he said unto her, Daughter, thy faith hath made thee whole; go in peace, and be whole of thy plague. (Mark 5:34)

2. But I will restore you to health and heal your wounds , declares the Lord. (Jeremiah 30:17)

3. He gives power to the weak, and to those who have no might He increases strength. Those who wait on the Lord shall renew their strength; they shall mount up with wings like eagles, they shall run and not be weary, they shall walk and not faint. (Isaiah 40: 29 & 31)

4. Heal me, O Lord, and I shall be healed; save me and I shall be saved, for you are my praise. (Jeremiah 17:14)

PRAYER FOR DELIVERANCE

Dear God,

We thank you, father, for what you are doing in our lives. God, we come to you in prayer now seeking your hands upon our lives. We ask for your guidance in areas where we were uncertain in the victories.

God, we seek your face and your will for our lives. We are asking that in areas you are cleaning up, God have your way. God, please heal us from our deepest and darkest pains.

Father, wherever the enemy may be lurking, we come now to dismantle every attack, every plot, every distraction, every place where he may lie, and God, we ask that you be our refuge.

God, send us to dwell in your secret place, knowing that right there is where you are. I love you and say, Father, have your way, to allow your will to be done.
In Jesus Name.
Amen!

3 WOUNDED WARRIOR

A woman is often the heartbeat of her family. The presence of a woman fills the room with power. Women have been responsible for being the glue that keeps everything from falling apart in the home. The magnitude of weight that we carry is often overlooked and misunderstood. As women, we find ourselves juggling multiple roles at one time. We have to find a way for our dreams and responsibilities to co-exist. I can reflect on when I was pursuing my Master's degree. There were days that I was balancing a nine-hour workday, homework, and family life. I wanted more for myself, but there were moments when it seemed impossible. After a long day of work, I would take my children to their after-school sports activities, sit outside, and complete my homework. Some days I didn't have time to do my homework because I was the team mom. Trying to keep the team organized was a big task to take on.

I always found myself saying yes to everything. Rarely did I carve out time just for myself.

Deep down, I was screaming, but I did everything with a smile on my face. However, my reality was that I needed a break, but I didn't know how to take a break. My child loved the idea that his mother was helping to keep his team together. I told myself if I stopped, then I would be letting my son down. I now know that wasn't true, but at that moment, the thought of it made me feel selfish.

I was so good at conjuring up a smile, even with a broken spirit. I did everything in my power to hide the pain and exhaustion that I felt. Although I did my best to ignore how I was feeling, I couldn't help but notice that my patterns took a toll on me. I began to take a mental note that, throughout each day. I was what everyone else needed; A mother, wife, friend, sister, best friend, co-worker, boss, entrepreneur, auntie, etc. However, I wasn't what I needed. Each role comes with great responsibility. Many people would look at all I was doing as; care, purpose, passion, love, concern, protection, victory, and perseverance. However, while I provided all of those things to others, it was simultaneously self-destructive. Deep down inside, I was experiencing pain, brokenness, battle wounds, failure, tiredness, rejection, self-ridicule, unhealthy people-pleasing habits, and personal defeat.

I became a wounded warrior without even noticing it. I wanted to make sure that the world I carried on my shoulders around me stayed put together. However, I took care of the world around me at the expense of taking care of myself. I didn't want anyone to know that I had become mentally and physically exhausted.

There were nights I would sit in my room and cry because

I wanted to rest mentally, but my goal of completing my degree required my time and attention. I wanted to prove to myself that, just because I became a mother at a younger age than I planned, I wouldn't let it interfere with my goals. Being a mother is rewarding, but we do not have to forget about ourselves in the process. I thought that my role as a mother meant I had to forfeit my dreams for so long. THAT IS NOT TRUE! To all of my mothers reading this book, I know it gets hard, and I know there are days when we run out of hours, but don't forfeit your dreams. You may have to accomplish your goals tired and frustrated, but you can do it!

How many of you reading this are in a "don't quit season?" You can't give up here. You need a small circle that reminds you, "don't quit here!" You may have to take a break, you may have to cry, but you cannot quit. We all have to set aside time to take care of our dreams and ourselves. When we throw away our dreams to take care of others, we become wounded warriors. Taking care of everyone else and neglecting you leads to brokenness. Yes, you will have to make sacrifices. Yes, you may have to change your timeline. However, you can still fulfill your dreams.

It may seem easier to quit fighting than to push through. Pushing through brings about the greater reward. Sis, the reward comes with your push. If you stop now, you will have to heal later. I'd rather fight through long days now than heal my broken heart later for giving up on me. It's okay if you have to pause or take a break as long as you don't quit. To all of my beautiful mothers who are reading this and, you have given up, get back in the game. As long as you have breath in your body, you can still fulfill your dreams. It may look a little different now, but you can still do it.

God is not intimidated by our circumstances. What is impossible to us is possible with God. "All things are possible if you believe." –Make 9:23 Jesus, the Good Shepherd, wants to order the steps of your life, guiding you safely through the valleys, over the mountains, and down the path of righteousness. God wants you to allow him to lead your paths. You don't have to do it all on your own. You don't have to be everything to everyone. The things that are too heavy for you, give them to God. Trust that he has a divine plan for your life. Proverbs 3:5–6 says, "Trust in the Lord with all your heart and do not rely on your own understanding. Acknowledge him in all your ways, and he will make your paths straight."

God wants you to allow him to be the driver in your life. Have you learned to trust God to handle things in your season of being down and frustrated? When I began to pray for God to intervene, I noticed that he begins to show up. Prayer was the step that I was missing. I was in my favorite superwoman cape once again, trying to do it all on my own. God kept tapping me on the shoulder, reminding me to take off my superwoman cape. I was making a mess of my life because I was trying to do my job and his.

Prayer is the answer to the weight of life. Prayer is the answer to your promise. Prayer allows God to make a way out of no way. Prayer allows us to find rest in him. Prayer has the power to shift your circumstances and your mindset.

Prayer has been my secret weapon when I was fighting battles that I couldn't win independently. There have been so many times where I've been too weak during a battle, but God gave me strength through prayer. Prayer goes beyond tears, frustration, and exhaustion. Prayer creates the atmosphere for God to abide in your situation. I've learned that sometimes God has to bring us to our knees so that he can show us that He is God. "And he said unto me, My grace is sufficient for thee: for my strength is made perfect in weakness. Most gladly, therefore, will I rather glory in my infirmities, that the power of Christ may rest upon me." 2 Corinthians 12:9 KJV. God will show himself through his power and glory. In our weakness, we find the courage and the strength to become more obedient. Why is that? In our weakness, we are more likely to make room for God. When everything is going well, we have a terrible habit of not making time for God. But the moment things fall apart, we find ourselves in the posture of prayer.

"You will seek me and find me when you seek me with all

your heart." –Jeremiah 29:13

when you seek God for the divine direction, He will change the trajectory of your life. I believe we hear God differently when we make prayer a part of our daily lives.

SCRIPTURES

1. Praise be to the God and Father of our Lord Jesus Christ, the Father of compassion and the God of all comfort, who comforts us in all our troubles, so that we can comfort those in any trouble with the comfort we ourselves receive from God. (2 Corinthians 1:3)

2. I have told you these things, so that in me you may have peace. In this world you will have trouble. But take heart! I have overcome the world. (John 16:33)

3. I remain confident of this: I will see the goodness of the LORD in the land of the living. Wait for the LORD; be strong and take heart and wait for the LORD. (Psalm 27:13-14)

4. In all these things we are more than conquerors through him who loved us. For I am convinced that neither death nor life, neither angels nor demons, neither the present nor the future, nor any powers, neither height nor depth, nor anything else in all creation, will be able to separate us from the love of God that is in Christ Jesus our Lord. (Romans 8:37-38)

PRAYER FOR STRENGTH

Dear God,

God, this is your daughter here at your feet.

Thank you for allowing me to see your wonderful works. God, thank you for getting me through my worst days so that I may be an example to others. God, thank you for not leaving me when I needed you most. Thank you for sharing the load with me. Thank you for subsiding my pain and shining your light upon me.

I trust you to take me from this place to the next. God, I pray that you will order my steps. I trust that you will guide me.

Would you please continue to speak to my heart and lead me in your holy way? God let me not become weary in well doing. Would you please give me the strength for all that lies ahead?

In Jesus Name.
Amen.

4 PRAYER WARRIOR

Your prayer life is what builds a strong relationship with God. As his daughter, there should be a strong desire to get to know God intimately. There are no conversations that are off-limit with our heavenly father. His desire is for you to make him a priority in your life. "And pray in the Spirit on all occasions with all kinds of prayers and requests. With this in mind, be alert and always keep on praying for all the Lord's people. –Ephesians 6:18.

Prayers can open doors that no man can shut. Therefore, as prayer warriors, we can find ourselves in constant communication with God. Prayer warriors also have an opportunity to lift others in prayer during our time with God. The very thing we need to know about prayer is, it is not a monologue; prayer is a dialogue. Prayer is not where we do all the talking, and God listens or sits back to take notes. It's where God has a conversation with us. "Call to me, and I will answer you, and will tell you great and hidden things that you have not known." –Jeremiah 33:3. There are many times when I sit in prayer and talk with God, and there are other times when I sit in his presence and wait for him to speak to me. I have open communication with God. I pray about things I need God to do, fix, change, shift, turn around, or manifest. When I become vulnerable with God, I begin seeing him work. We do not have to come to God perfect we have to go before him with an open heart. There are times when my Spirit is too heavy to get words out, and I cry out to God, and he understands the prayers of my heart. There have also been moments when I have come to God angry and frustrated, and he understands my emotions. I am so grateful that God doesn't require a filter before he accepts us. He wants us to come to him with our deepest and darkest secrets. He doesn't want us to hide the ugly parts of our story from him. He welcomes you and all of your problems into his presence.

Prayer is how we invite the supernatural presence of the Almighty to invade our life. Prayer is where we take time to learn how God effectively communicates with us. Prayer is where we get to hear exciting things when we stop talking and start listening. Not only do we get the opportunity to speak to Him, but God very dearly wants to speak to you also. The vital aspect of prayer is before you get off your knees, have a moment with God, and make sure you listen for the instructions after the prayer. If we are praying for direction and guidance, we must remain still long enough to hear God's response and direction. If we are praying for God to usher our footsteps, we must listen for the steps and the path to take. When in prayer and you are asking God for wisdom and understanding about a relationship. Prayer and listening go hand in hand. Prayer also allows us to become one with the voice of God. The opening of our spirits to his voice will enable us to become more familiar with his voice. The Bible teaches us: "This is the confidence we have in approaching God: that if we ask anything according to his will, he hears us." -1 John 5:14. God wants us to be confident when we pray. Confidence is having or showing assurance. Confidence in our prayers is without question, we know that God will answer our prayers if they are according to his will. Our confidence in our prayers is an example of our faith. "Therefore, I tell you, whatever you ask in prayer, believe that you have received it, and it will be yours. –Mark 11:24.

Prayer that breaks Yokes

What would happen if you decided right now that you would do everything in your power to make today count for something? What if you chose to wake up and begin the fight for your purpose? What if you decided that it wasn't just going to be another prayer when you prayed, but it was going to be a prayer that makes a difference? Prayer is part of your birthright. When you take the opportunity to come before God, make sure you come boldly and make it a prayer of power. Make it a prayer of absolute surrender. Release whatever has been weighing you down. Prayer is the key that will unlock your blessings. In the unlocking is where the enemy gets busy. Satan knows once you began to unlock what God has for you, you've gained access to the power and authority of what belongs to you. God has assigned particular blessings to you, and the enemy doesn't want you to have those things. However, when you pray, not only will you make your request known, but God will give you instructions to provide you with power over the enemy.

Use your power as a moment to pull down spiritual strongholds and powers and principalities that are set against you. Use it to bind what is coming against you. Use prayer to cover your family. Use the power of prayer to push past distractions that are sent to pull you away from destiny. Use prayer to conquer sickness in your body. Use it to defeat the giants that are standing against you. Use it to move heaven and earth. When you open your mouth to pray with confidence that God will answer your prayers.

SCRIPTURES

1. Devote yourselves to prayer, being watchful and thankful. (Colossians 4:2)

2. Call to me and I will answer you and tell you great and unsearchable things you do not know. (Jeremiah 33:3)

3. Let us then approach God's throne of grace with confidence, so that we may receive mercy and find grace to help us in our time of need. (Hebrew 4:16)

4. You did not choose me, but I chose you and appointed you so that you might go and bear fruit; fruit that will last; and so that whatever you ask in my name the father will give you. (John 15:16)

PRAYER FOR COVERING

Heavenly Father,

I am approaching your throne with an open heart. God, I may not have all the right words to say, but please look into my heart. God, please prepare me for the battle ahead. I want to move forward knowing that you are with me.

Guide me and provide me with divine instructions and plans to defeat the enemy. Father, I need you to provide clarity where I lack understanding.

God give me strength and help me to remember "greater is he that is in me, than he that is in the world." Would you please dismantle any attack of the enemy and cover me in your precious blood?

God, I will walk in faith, knowing you have sent your angels to protect me on my assignments. Thank you for trusting me.

I love you.
In Jesus Name.

5 ACTIVATING FAITH

When hard times come, and it seems God is deviating from the plan, we can feel disconnected from God. Have you ever asked God if he has forgotten about you? Or have you ever asked God can he still hear your prayers? How quickly do we forget that God is in control? We say, God, I trust you all the time, but when things don't go as planned, we question the one who created the plan. Usually, we begin to grow frustrated when we no longer seem to be on schedule.

Our faith is not developed as a result of everything

going our way. Instead, it's in the moments of uncertainty when we must exercise our faith. "I am sure of this, that He who started a good work in you will carry it on to completion until the day of Christ Jesus." –Philippians 1:6. What I love about this text is that God is stating a promise. Everything he has started, he must see it to the end. This promise shows me that no matter what road I take, we will arrive at the promises of God. Have you ever been on your way to visit friends and family, but on the way there, you had to take a detour? Detours can be unsettling because usually, the road is unfamiliar. When we aren't accustomed to the road, we tend to pay more attention to where we are going. Sometimes God sends us on a detour so that he can have our undivided attention. He knows that if we don't know where we are going, we have no other choice than to follow him to our destination. Detours can throw off your plan, but the destination doesn't change. We must learn to trust God even when we have to take a spiritual detour.

I've also learned that every delay doesn't result in a detour.

Sometimes there is something that is being rectified ahead that is slowing down our process. Living in Atlanta, there is always an accident or ongoing roadwork, leading to horrible traffic. It doesn't matter if I wake up on time and get all of the boys dressed and out the door; I still find myself running late because the road leading to my destination is unpredictable. Just when I think that everything is running smoothly, traffic begins to slow down, and before I know it, I'm sitting in bumper-to-bumper traffic. I usually get anxious, and I try to look ahead to see if I can figure out the cause of the delay. No matter how anxious I get or how many times I hunk my horn, I'm not able to make the trip any faster. Once traffic begins moving, I'm usually able to see the cause for the delay. Sometimes a car is being towed, and a lane has been closed to clean up remnants of an accident. Other times there has been a lane closed to fix the horrible potholes on the highway. Despite the cause for the delay, I always make it to the destination even if it's not at my desired time. The wait felt like an inconvenience, but it was really protection. I could have been the person in the car accident, or I could have hit a pothole and burst my tire. But by the grace of God, I didn't. The delay was rectifying something that I would bypass in my process. If you only knew all of the things that God allowed you to bypass in your process you would find yourself being thankful instead of complaining.

I know for a fact that when I stopped trying to make my own plans work, God began to show me the plans that he had for me. We must activate our faith in moments of uncertainty. We need faith to follow the plan of God. If we don't have faith, we will ignore what God is telling us to do.

Who leads you as a prayer warrior? Our spiritual commander and chief, Jesus Christ. Jesus has saved you from the hands of the enemy who wanted charge over you. When you choose to stand on the side with God, you are given a more powerful power than any plan of the enemy. You have been given dominion of the fowls of the air and over the beast of the sea. Follow his leading, and he will never lead you astray.

There are so many biblical accountants where God has shown us how to move in prayer through our savior. Jesus starts with, "I pray not for the world," meaning the carnal(flesh) unbelieving part of the world. He prayed here as an advocate for the believers, those who believe in who he is and what he was sent here to do, making intercession and making a spiritual way for those who trust and stand in his father. " When we trust God, we have access to the will of God. When we are in the wheel of God, then we are protected by God. The enemy can't destroy God's plans for your life.

Sis, let this serve as a reminder that you Are the Daughter of the Most High God! He hears your prayers. We have a mediator sent on our behalf to ensure that what we are asking reaches heaven. You must trust what he tells you to do. In the previous chapter I talked about prayer not just being about your request but also God's response to your request.

I believe that in all things, God leads an army of angels

that has an assignment to go before us in battle. The angels are assigned to fight on your behalf. The other army is the intercessors and prayer warriors that have been given power and authority to pray and submit on your behalf. "For he shall give his angels charge over thee, to keep thee in all thy ways. They shall bear thee up in their hands, lest thou dash thy foot against a stone." –Psalms 91:11-12. God has set before us in this text a promise from him.

His promise is that the same way the angels surrounded Elisha and his servant and ensured their protection, God has given the same charge over our lives. God has sent our angels to protect us, watch over us, divine protection. It is down in the marching orders of the hosts of heaven that they take special note of the people who dwell in God and those that diligently seek him. When we trust God, we are protected from things that we can't even begin to comprehend.

SCRIPTURES

1. And Jesus answered them, "Have faith in God. Truly, I say to you, whoever says to this mountain, Be taken up and thrown into the sea, and does not doubt in his heart, but believes that what he says will come to pass, it will be done for him. Therefore I tell you, whatever you ask in prayer, believe that you have received it, and it will be yours. (Mark 11: 22-24)

2. For I consider that the sufferings of this present time are not worth comparing with the glory that is to be revealed to us. (Romans 8:18)

3. And without faith it is impossible to please God, because anyone who comes to him must believe that he exists and that he rewards those who earnestly seek him. (Hebrews 11:6)

4. If you believe, you will receive whatever you ask for in prayer. (Matthew 21:22)

PRAYER OF FAITH

Heavenly Father,

I come to you with a special request. God, there are times when I try to fix things on my own. God, please help me to relinquish control. I know that I can do nothing without your help.

I know that you can see things that are before me. So I am coming to you asking that you will guide me.

Father, I need your help.
God, I don't want to walk this road alone. You said in your word, "without faith; it is impossible to please you." God, I desire to please you in everything that I do. Would you please help my unbelief?

God, I vow to trust in all things from this day forward. Thank you for hearing my prayer.

I love you.

In Jesus Name.
Amen

6 PREPERATION

When a major snowstorm comes, what do you do? Most run to the grocery store to stock up on food, water, and candles just in case we're stuck in the house for a few days. Why do we go and buy up all the bread and milk? You don't want to be stuck in the house without anything to eat if you're like me. Back in 2014, Atlanta had a snowstorm. The kids went to school that morning, parents to work as if it was a normal weekday. By mid-afternoon, the entire city was in a panic by noon. There was a storm coming that we weren't prepared for. Schools were calling for parents to come and pick up students. Company's allowed employees to leave early. Highways were backed up, stores were crowded, and shelves were empty. The unexpected storm was followed by a string of unexpected events. The storm led to unexpected road closures, flooding, power outages, and unwarranted stress.

Life can throw some unexpected storms in our paths. Sometimes those storms come with unforeseen obstacles that require extreme cleanup. During the storm, we began wishing that we had come more prepared. We start thinking about the generator and flashlights that we walked past while we were in Home Depot. We start to second guess if we bought enough water and nonperishable items while during our store run. When we focus on our lack of preparation, fear settles in, and anxiety shows up. We start to panic because we are not sure how we are going to survive the storm. We began to think of ways to pull ourselves out of the storm and go into survival mode. Preparation helps to minimize the stress and anxiety of the survival process.

I can pose the question, why don't we prepare? Some will respond by saying, "We didn't know the storm was coming." Most would say, "Had I known the storm would be this bad, I would have taken time out to stock up more or have done more if I had known the storm would last this long." Others would reply, "I didn't have enough time to get prepared because there were so many things I had to do to prepare for the storm." Which would be your response? My response would probably be, "I didn't have enough time to get prepared." I am known for getting things done, but I have to admit sometimes I procrastinate. There are times when I am unsure of what God is instructing me to do, or I'll wait until the last minute to move because I'm trying to figure everything out. I love fulfilling a task, but there are times when I struggle to get started. I can watch the weather report, and I'll find myself saying I need to go to the store, but I may wait until the morning of, before I start preparing. The fact of the matter is we don't always have time to get prepared. Like the 2014 snowstorm, many schools, companies, and individuals did not prepare for the storm. Procrastinating put so many people in difficult positions. As a prayer warrior, we can't wait for the storm to come before we start praying. We must prepare for the storms by strengthening our relationship with God when everything is running smoothly.

As a mother, there is always something to complete or something that needs my attention. As a wife, there's always a position that requires my attention. As a friend, there will always be some who needs a listening ear and support. We try to make sure no one feels left out or unsure if we are committed to our word in every role. It is my responsibility to fulfill my duties as a wife, mother, and friend before the storm arises. If I am in constant communication with my husband, then I know what to pray for. I'm not waiting for a challenge to show up in our home before I cover my family. The same goes for my children and my friendships. Are you taking time to cover yourself in prayer and seeking God

DAILY to prepare for whatever comes your way?

When we come to battle empty-handed and not

prepared, we become subject to the enemy's schemes. One

thing about the enemy, he is always ready. He remains

focused on the battlefield. He already knows what tricks to

use to stir you up. He knows the weakened areas of your life

and how to test your faith. He comes with the manuscript on

how to get you off course. He knows the imperfections that

God is working on in you. So why leave your future up to

him? Let me give you an example; knowing that I had so

many things on my plate to do, I knew that I must have

things written out because if I did not, I would forget. I

would have an important meeting with my non-profit

women's organization. If I didn't schedule it on my calendar,

I would forget to start the meeting. There would be times; my

co-president would call me to ensure that I was ready. I

would laugh off my nervous energy, but the reality was, I was

tired and simply forgot. Therefore, I had to come up with a

better plan for execution. The plan needed to ensure that I was prepared for what was ahead.

The battle plan is essential in making sure you prepare yourself for what's to come. It can be challenging preparing for something that you don't see coming. When it's sunny outside, it doesn't make sense to go and buy an umbrella, but the rain will eventually come. God instructs us on how to prepare for the storms that we don't see coming. Ephesians 6:12, "For we do not wrestle against flesh and blood, but against the rulers, against the authorities, against the cosmic powers over this present darkness, against the spiritual forces of evil in the heavenly places." This place is complex and sometimes unstable. It can feel like you're doing too much. Has anyone ever said to you, girl, you are doing way too much? Doing seasons of preparation, you can't afford to listen to those who don't fully understand your assignment. There will be people around you that will try to talk you out of preparing. The reason being is not everyone understands the importance of preparation. It is essential to have an intimate relationship with God. He will provide you with discernment to see beyond your circumstances. Our communication with God is vital for our preparation for the storm. Each battle plan becomes your layout and your instructions for the battle. It's the place where you begin to prepare. Therefore, you should never go into battle unprepared. When Jesus started to ascend to heaven, he left a battle plan. He gave specific thought and instructions. John 14:3 states, "And if I go and prepare a place for you, I will come back and take you to be with me that you also may be where I am." (NLT) Jesus is making a bold statement that he left to prepare a place for us by His death. The High Priest, in the ancient ritual, once a year was privileged to lift the heavy veil and pass into the dark chamber. There was only the light between the cherubim. Even in the bible, there were periods of darkness. However, the new testament speaks of the power of fellowship with God. The realization of the most intimate fellowship with heavenly things and communion with God is made possible because Jesus has died. Here in the text, we can see how the battle plan becomes the layout

of our victory. Jesus died on the cross for our victory. The

cross was hard for Jesus. He cried out to God, "why has thou

forsaken me?" The ultimate sacrifice was made during the

darkest moment of Jesus' life. God never promised in his

word that we wouldn't face trials and tribulations, but he did

promise, "The weapons formed against us would not

prosper." He also promised us that he would be there with

us, uphold us, strengthen us, and sustain us. We can look at

the disciples, the prophets, and even Jesus's life to see this

truth in this very thought. They all came face to face with the

enemy at some point in their walks.

I wish that being a daughter of God exempted us

from the storms of life, but that isn't how it works. We all

have to go through some unfavorable circumstances. We

don't have complete control over the hand we are dealt.

However, we do have the power to prepare to the best of our

ability. Preparation may not stop the pain or prevent the storm, but it can save our lives during the storm.

We sometimes forget that we are not in control as much as we would like to be. So, what are we supposed to do to prepare? Where do we go? How do we prepare ourselves? The first step is to realize that preparation comes when we build our foundation on solid ground with Jesus as our guide and source of strength. If we are going to grow deeper in our faith and have a strong foundation, we must spend time building a relationship with the Lord. What if you choose to believe God? We should turn to him and allow him to guide our thoughts, actions, and our walk. We should cling to his word and use it as an everyday source and weapon during battle. We should adhere to Him as though our life depends on it. We desperately need Jesus every step of the way.

When we look at how military soldiers prepare for battle, it's a remarkable area to notice. There is a specific uniform, shoe, and walk. There is a confident demeanor that carries along with a soldier. New soldiers do not know what to expect and don't know what to ask or do initially. There is a training process that ALL new soldiers must go through. There is stripping of old ways and old behavior. "The old man cannot be carried into a new lifestyle." Look at how profound that statement is. We cannot meet God at our next level until we break away from our old selves. We cannot get on the battlefield with our old ways of fighting. Carnal fighting is not the same thing as spiritual fighting. As a child of God, we must stand on the battlefield with spiritual eyes, mindset, clothing, and weapons. The training that new soldiers go through gives them an idea of what to expect. It also prepares them mentally for what's ahead. A Sargent in the military has the assignment of making sure they prepare a soldier for deployment. There is not only mental training. There's also physical training to prepare the body as well. There is a test that helps them through the rigors of Basic Combat Training. I think battle mind helps outline some critical areas that will better prepare Soldiers before they deploy. This way, the Soldiers don't feel alone when they are in combat. The same is true for the spiritual battles that we face. There is training that has to take place. God is our Commander and Chief, and he gets us in shape before we go into battle. Another form of preparation is to become an active follower of Christ. One common term was "Followers of the Way." Some used the term "witness." Yet, the most common term for those who we now call Christians as disciples. Disciple means follower; in other words, we follow Christ. Following Christ indeed involves a wholehearted commitment. It requires that we surrender. We must surrender our entire being to God so that he can have complete control in our lives. We cannot see a relationship with Christ as simply a ticket into heaven but merely the beginning of a process. We can't follow Christ until we accept him being the leading force in our lives.

Some use the quote, "Allow God to become the driving force in your life." Allowing him to be the center and the push button of our faith. As a devote Christian, this background becomes solid and essential in our lives. We must truly understand what it means to follow Christ. Create a new routine that involves spending quality time with God in his word and with prayer. "Create in me a clean heart, Oh God; and renew a right spirit within me." –Psalm 51:10.

To become faithful followers of Christ and His gospel, we must deny ourselves daily. Lay down the things that are not like him and adopt his will. Is this part of the battle plan? Absolutely! When we deny ourselves, it causes us to become disciplined. It allows us to look in the mirror and accept the things about us that we need to change. We cannot go into battle partially prepared. Partial preparation makes you an easier target. You can't fight a battle if you are broken and in pieces. A soldier can't be on the frontline with a broken riffle. As followers of Christ, we must do more than wake up and go to church every bible study and Sunday service. Becoming a faithful follower is a lifestyle adjustment. We have to seek God for ourselves. At the beginning of 2020, none of us could have predicted that we would no longer be able to gather for worship. Many of us who were used to going to church every Sunday morning suddenly didn't have that option. We no longer were able to rely on going to church. We had to invest in our personal relationships with God. You began praying more, not only for yourself but also for others. We were in a battle with little to no preparation.

Another step in the battle process to be a follower of Christ is to make sure your inner circle is faith-filled. Who surrounds you in a storm or in the heart of a battle is crucial. My Pastor, Dier Hopkins, has focused our church on the level of unity. We should never voyage alone in the walk; it's a trick and disguise of the enemy. Nor is this process a desire from God. God did not create us to walk in this life alone. He desires for us to connect and build solid foundations with other leaders and believers. This bond creates the fort needed in battle. We are stronger when two or more touch and agree upon something. Two are better than one in warfare. 1 Thessalonians 5:11 states, "Therefore encourage one another and build up one another, just as you also are doing." As a unit, we can teach each other, encourage each other, and build one another up. We can correct each other, rebuke each other, and pray for one another on many levels. God's plan and his design for the church is that Christ be the head and we are to be the body. We need to connect ourselves to the head of the body for us to function. Acts 2:42 reads, "They were continually devoting themselves to the apostles' teaching and to fellowship, to the breaking of bread and to prayer." Within this bracket, it's always good to have an accountability partner. The accountability partner is a friend/person that you can walk beside you. As women, we have to get together and hold each other accountable.

You need sisters in your corner who will lift you when you are broken and challenge you to strive for excellence when mediocrity has settled in. Surround yourself with strong women of faith. These women will remind you of the word and promises of God when the storm has caused darkness to overshadow your faith. We all find ourselves in dark places where we can no longer envision the promises of God. You should see a strong connection where you can be vulnerable and honest. You aren't always going to feel blessed and highly favored. Some days you may feel lost and confused. In these moments, you will need prayer warriors to cover you. You need a friend that can hold you accountable when you mess up and encourage you in your walk with God.

A mentor in Christ would be similar in this setting as well. A mentor is typically someone that can pour into you and guide you as you walk through life. A mentor has already been down your path. They have already conquered your journey. A mentor has already walked through the stage of life you are in and can help guide you down the chartered paths of life with God. Above all these things, you need someone who will stand with you in prayer. They will push you towards greatness. Prayer is the key to open doors and gives you victory in battles that you didn't see coming. Prayer ushers you in the direction to hear God during the battle. We should all be connected to prayer warriors.

<u>SCRIPTURES</u>

1. Behold, I send an angel before you to guard you on the way and to bring you to the place that I have prepared. (Exodus 23:20)

2. And we know that for those who love God all things work together for good, for those who are called according to his purpose. (Romans 8:28)

3. Preach the word; be ready in season and out of season; reprove, rebuke, and exhort, with complete patience and teaching (2 Timothy 4:2)

4. But in your hearts honor Christ the Lord as holy, always being prepared to make a defense to anyone who ask you for a reason for the hope that is in you; yet do it with gentleness and respect (1 Peter 3:15)

PRAYER OF GUIDANCE

Heavenly Father,
I am approaching you in need of your guidance. God, I don't know all you have for my life, but I trust you. God, please prepare me for all that you have in store for me. I want to move forward in pure confidence that you order my steps.

Guide me through every storm and every battle.
Father, I need you to prepare me for greatness.

God give me the strength to never give up. Would you please give me the courage to trust you will when it doesn't make sense? Would you please protect me and cover me as I encounter spiritual warfare.

God, I will walk in faith, knowing that the enemy will not defeat me. Thank you for choosing me for this assignment.

I love you.

In Jesus Name.
Amen

7 SPIRITUAL STRENGTH

Do you work out regularly? Do you work out to look good or because you want to get stronger? I have to be honest; when I do work out, it's mainly for esthetic purposes. Growing up, I struggled with my appearance. I desired to look a certain way, thinking, I thought my image would help me become more popular with the crowds and easily fit in. I was always a small frame woman, so I never worked out to lose weight, but I had other insecurities that I wanted to fix. I struggled to put weight on, and I struggled to keep weight on as I encountered stressful situations.

When I went through my divorce, the process took a toll on me. At the time, I was in my early twenties, and I was a fairly new mother. I struggled with my reality of becoming a single mother. The stress I endured negatively impacted my body. The stress caused me to lose my appetite completely, and I struggled to eat. Eating was a thing I had to force myself to do for 6-7 years. As I continuously lost weight, I became very insecure about my body. I used to sit back and listen to women complain about losing weight and how much they hated having weight-hanging. I would sit and listen desperately, wishing that I could somehow take their weight and add it to my body. People would criticize my weight by commenting how I needed to eat because I was so skinny, not knowing that eating was a challenge. Eating would make me physically sick. It was challenging to force myself to consume nutrients for my body. My physical weight began dropping, but my emotional weight became nearly unbearable.

Can you imagine what it would be like to walk around for 24 hours carrying 100lb weights? Imagine not being able to take a break or put the weights down for an entire day. Now imagine trying to cover up the sweat that was running down your face. Or better yet, imagine keeping a smile on your face while you're carrying 100 extra pounds weights. Think about how the weights would occupy your mind. Every time you want to do something, you are reminded that you aren't free because you are carrying around weight that is no longer serving you. This is how I felt. The weight of my circumstances made it difficult for me to pretend that everything was okay with me. It took so much strength to hid the discomfort, and it took even more strength to muster up a smile. I was flat-out exhausted.

I finally became fed up, and I decided that something had to change. I realized being tired and carrying around dead weight was no longer an option. I had a relationship with God, but I cared more about how the relationship looked. Meanwhile, I didn't intimately know God. I claimed to know

God, but the truth is I was lost and nervous because life was not happening the way I had planned it. Life was not giving me what I was putting out. I was full of fear and low self-esteem. I didn't want anyone to recognize that I was struggling because I had an image to uphold. But one day, after working a long day at work, I came home and found myself exhausted. I couldn't pretend anymore. I needed a supernatural encounter with God. I knew that the only way to get to a place of fulfillment was by strengthening my relationship with God. It was time for me to stop focusing on the esthetics of my relationship with God. Instead, I needed to focus on strengthening my relationship with God. "Therefore, my dear friends, as you have always obeyed not only in my presence but now much more in my absence, continue to work out your salvation with fear and trembling, for it is God who works in you to will and to act in order to fulfill his good purpose." –Philippians 2: 12-13.

If we don't work out physically, we find decreased strength within our bodies. Some can't miss a day of working out because it provides therapeutic provisions for their lives and their day. The same happens spiritually. When we stop working out spiritually, we become weak, and we also find ourselves struggling to get through the day. In the same way, we need exercise for our physical muscles; our spiritual muscles need to be worked out as well. That spiritual workout is necessary to ensure that we withstand the adversities of life. We must be strong in our faith to withstand the hard blows that are thrown our way. A spiritual workout consists of praying, fasting, reading your word, praise and worship. It also consists of loving your neighbor, showing kindness, and helping those in need. We need a good balance of all of those things to stay in shape spiritually.

How are you doing working out spiritually? What spiritual muscles are you targeting? If love is a weak spiritual muscle, what are you doing to make it stronger? Serving, helping those in need, and showing kindness are ways that you can increase your spiritual muscles pertaining to love. Perhaps forgiveness is a spiritual muscle that you need to target. What are you working on to strengthen that muscle? Take a survey over your life, evaluate the people whom you still allow power over because you haven't forgiven them. Start exercising that muscle by finding the power to forgive those who have deeply hurt you. Release what they have done to you and cry out to God. You may not always have the opportunity to have a conversation with the person that has hurt you. Still, you can always have a conversation with God. You do not have to carry around the pain of your past. Release your pain through prayer and worship. When we dwell in the presence of God, he provides healing for our souls. The Bible says, "For if ye forgive men their trespasses, your heavenly Father will also forgive you:" –Matthew 6:14. I don't know about you, but I always need to be in the seat of forgiveness with the father. I never want to be in a position where God does not forgive me because I won't/refuse to forgive others.

I understand that forgiveness isn't always the easy thing to do. Sometimes the pain is so great until it feels impossible.

You must first open your heart to the idea of forgiveness. You can't allow forgiveness into your heart if it's closed. Pray and ask God to help first open your heart. Prayer for healing from the un-forgiveness is where your freedom resides. God wants his daughters to be free in him. You take your power back when you forgive.

What about strengthening your spiritual muscles in the area of giving? Do you find yourself being selfish, or do you freely give? When writing about this very thought, God wanted me to stop and check my heart first. While writing this, some things were assigned to my sinful state of mind that I wanted God to compromise on. In my selfishness, I tried to bargain with God. I wanted God to see past this thorn and see that I have the heart that yearns for him. I tried to negotiate with God, explaining that there is never a time I didn't want to be used, but this thorn, "God please don't remove this bit of pleasure, sinful pleasure, but I will serve you, just look away." The spiritual muscle in the area of giving is strengthened when we say yes to God. We have first to give

God our life and let him take control of it. I know it's tough to hand everything over to God when you think you've got it all planned out. My selfishness kept me thinking that my current feet were still following God because I didn't want to give up what was in my left hand, but rather what was in my right hand was all God. I was selfish in wanting God to look over my imperfections for my own satisfaction.

God wants purity in our hearts. We don't have to be perfect, but we must be pure in heart. I believe God loves us so much that when we come to him with our imperfections, he will help us work through them. His grace is sufficient. God, our creator, created us in his image, and in that image, it is perfected in his eyes. "His strength is made perfect in our weakness." -2 Corinthians 12:9.

<u>Strength & Courage</u>

"And whatsoever we ask, we receive of him, because we keep his commandments, and do those things that are pleasing in his sight." 1 John 3:22 KJV

Be Strong and Courageous! There were several places in the Bible where the daughters of God or the sons of God needed to be strong and courageous. David and Goliath, one of the most popular stories in the Bible, give us an example of strength and courage. David had to face a giant before he could win the battle. Judging by his outward appearance, it looked impossible for him to win. He was looked over in his conquest to be selected to battle against this giant. As the Philistine moved closer to attack him, David sprinted toward the battle line to meet him. Reaching into his bag and taking out a stone, he slung it and struck the Philistine on the forehead? The stone sank into his forehead, and he fell face down on the ground. 1Samuel 17: 48-49. David knew his strength before he was able to defeat the giant. Strength is measured in many ways; David's strength was the courage to know that he had all he needed to defeat the giant. David was able to push through the fear of what the giant looked like. He pushed past the audience of people surrounding him. He pushed past those who doubted him. David had to be strong and courageous. How do you know you are strong? You run to the battle line! You don't shrink. What Goliath is God calling you to take on? When we believe that God is working behind the scenes, it gives us courage and strength to overcome anything. Continue to strengthen your spiritual muscles and prepare for battle.

<u>SCRIPTURES</u>

1. So if you are offering your gift at the altar and there remember that your brother has something against you leave your gift there before the altar and go. First be reconciled to your brothers and then come and offer your gift. (Matthew 5:23-24)

2. For if you forgive other people when they sin against you, your heavenly father will also forgive you. (Matthew 6:14)

3. Love prospers when a fault is forgiven, but dwelling on it separates close friends. (Proverbs 17:9)

4. But I say to you who hear: love your enemies, do good to those who hate you. (Luke 6:27)

PRAYER OF FORGIVENESS

Father God,

We come humbly to you, asking you for you to give us strength. God, we need healing from those who hurt us. We need you to comfort our spirits and lift our heads. Heal our hearts from within. Purify our minds, cleanse our souls.

Please give us back our power and cleanse us from all unforgivable things done to us.

Would you please give us the ability to let go of the hurtful things that have been said to us? Would you please give us the strength to live and walk freely in you?

We repent for the un-forgiveness and ask you to shift us in a new direction.
We declare this prayer done!

In Jesus' precious name, we pray.
Amen!

8 MOVING FORWARD

Are you ready to move forward in life? Before God can completely transform your life, you must first decide to allow God to shed the old and birth the new. Moving forward means asking and seeking God for forgiveness in those areas that are no longer in alignment with God's will for your life. Repent for your sins. Repenting means turning away from sin and turning toward God, and obeying His word. When you repent of your sins, you make a conscious effort to deviate from your plans so that you can follow

God's plans.

During the process of moving forward, you will begin changing for the better. As you began to change will need to remain persistent in your pursuit to please God. Your decision to follow God doesn't make your life perfect, but it does ensure that you are in alignment. Some make the statement, "All Hell seems to break loose once I turn to Christ." The reason is that Satan feels as though he can entice you to move back and turn back into the direction of sin. The temptation becomes harder to resist. The change becomes harder to live in.

There are moments in the process that are more challenging than others. Sometimes you will feel very strong, and there are other times when you feel like it's too difficult. The truth is that it isn't always easy, but it's always worth it. "Therefore, since we are surrounded by such a great cloud of witnesses, let us throw off everything that hinders and the sin that so easily entangles. And let us run with perseverance the race marked out for us." –Hebrew 12:1. When you decide to follow God, you have to stay committed to doing life with Jesus. Even when you find yourself in dark moments and feel alone, you still have to remain committed. Yes, things will get hard, and yes, sometimes you may even want to give up, but you must stay the course.

Are you aware that you are an overcomer? As an overcomer, you must have faith. There will be moments when you will have to rely on your faith to get through challenging moments. The story that comes to mind concerning being a faith walker is the story of Elizabeth. Her story is an example of how faith pushes, births, and shift things in our lives.

Elizabeth was married to Zechariah, a priest. She was also known as the cousin to Mary, the mother of Jesus. The New Testament describes Elizabeth and her husband, Zechariah, as "righteous and blameless" people who observed "all the Lord's commands and decrees blamelessly." (Luke 1:6) We read that Elizabeth was barren, meaning she was unable to have children. When Zechariah was in the temple giving an offering to the Lord, Gabriel, the angel, appeared to him. The angel, Gabriel, said Zechariah and Elizabeth would soon be parents and that they would name their baby John. Zechariah found this a bit hard to believe since both he and his wife were "old." Gabriel told Zechariah that he wouldn't be able to speak until the prophecy was fulfilled in the birth of John. Soon, Elizabeth learns that she is pregnant.

When they first received the word, it seemed impossible. Have you ever received word from God that seemed impossible to manifest? The same was the case for Elizabeth and Zechariah. The only way they got to the place of manifestation was by believing. Literally, you see here that there had to be an unmeasured amount of faith to push forward. God needs you to believe and trust him no matter what. Not allowing your heart to be hardened while waiting on that promise or word spoken to manifest. In the wait, know that faith births perseverance, the ability to see and push past where you currently are.

When we decide to follow God, we are not only letting go of our ways but also putting ourselves in the best position to acquire the things that we desperately desire. Sometimes we find ourselves stuck because we allow ourselves to believe that we know better than God. As long as you continue doing things your way, you will find yourself living an unfulfilled life. However, when you decide to make the transition to follow God, you gain access to his strength, protection, and provision.

SCRIPTURES

1. Remember not the former things, nor consider the things of old. (Isaiah 43:18)

2. Therefore, if anyone is in Christ, he is a new creation. The old has passed away; behold, the new has come. (2 Corinthians 5:17)

3. I press on toward the goal for the prize of the upward call of God in Christ Jesus (Philippians 3:14)

4. Let your eyes look directly forward, and your gaze be straight before you. (Proverbs 4:25)

PRAYER OF PROGRESSION

Father,

We come to you bowing at your feet and seeking your face in prayer and your spirit with this supplication.

Thank you, father, for your forgiveness and your mercies. Thank you for not abandoning us in our mistakes and loving us through our imperfections.
We repent of those things that we have done knowingly and unknowingly in your sight. Cleanse our hearts. Heal the broken places that keep us from moving forward.

Would you please help us to be in alignment with your will for our lives? Would you please help us to trust your plan when we don't understand it? Turn us from our old ways and shift us t to a new way of living.

We thank you and love you. We believe in our hearts that you will answer our prayers.

In Jesus' name.
Amen!

9 PROTECTION

I consider myself to be a dedicated friend. I genuinely care about the well-being of my friends. I love to see them win, and I always want to see them grow. I want people around me to succeed as much as I want to succeed. My desire to see those that I love succeed has also caused me to become a fixer. I found myself wanting to fix every problem that my friends would encounter throughout their process. I was somehow convinced that I could protect them from going through hardships. I wanted to ensure that everyone was in a happy place, no matter the sacrifice. People would look and call me concerning every area of their lives. At the time, I didn't understand that the bumps and bruises of their process were necessary. I had to learn how to protect my friends without controlling them.

God also cares about our well-being, and he genuinely wants us to succeed in our purpose. He wants us to be victorious, but he also wants us to grow. There are times when we will have to go through challenging circumstances within our process. He will allow us to face adversities, but he will not allow the hardships to destroy us. God is the ultimate fixer, and he always steps in when we need him most. There are times when we want God to rescue us, but God understands that the hardships develop us for our purpose. Although we may experience pain, he continues to put a hedge of protection around us.

I am reminded of the story of Job. Job was a wealthy man, and the bible describes him as blameless and upright. God thought very highly of his servant Job. Satan tried to convince God that Job was righteous only because of God's favor. God knew that if he took away his favor, that his servant would still serve him. God allowed him to undergo great hardship because he knew that he could trust Job with trouble. Although he let all of Job's children tragically die, he still protected Job. Once things got too hard for Job to handle, God Intervened. Although Job experienced an astronomical amount of pain, God still covered him throughout the process.

We will see those we love go through great adversity as prayer warriors, but we must cover them in prayer. The greatest form of protection that we can offer to those we love is through prayer. I had to learn that it is not my responsibility to be a fixer as God's daughter. However, I did have the responsibility of praying over those who were going through difficult times. God is the fixer and the way-maker. We see Jesus in John 17:9 in the text where he prayed. "I pray for them. I am not praying for the world, but for those, you have given me, for they are yours." Here, Jesus interceded on behalf of his intercessors. As a daughter of God and a prayer warrior, when you go to God on behalf of others, Jesus will go to God on your behalf.

SCRIPTURES

1. So do not fear, for I am with you; do not be dismayed, for I am your God. I will strengthen you and help you; I will uphold you with my righteous right hand. (Isaiah 41:10)

2. Keep me safe, LORD, from the hands of the wicked; protect me from the violent, who devise ways to trip my feet. (Psalm 140:4)

3. We are hard pressed on every side, but not crushed; perplexed, but not in despair; persecuted but not abandoned; struck down, but not destroyed.
(2 Corinthians 4:8-9)

4. Put on the full armor of God, so that you can take your stand against the devil's schemes. (Ephesians 6:11)

PRAYER OF PROTECTION

Father God,

Thank you for your hedge of protection that surrounds me. Thank you for protecting me in times when I didn't even know I was in danger. Thank you, God, for choosing me to be a prayer warrior.

As I come to you lifting others in prayer, God, please, give me the words to say. God allow your angels to intercede on my behalf.

Thank you, God, for the victory over the enemy. Father, thank you for trusting me to lift my sisters in prayer.

I declare that you will cover me in your blood as I continue to fulfill my purpose.

In Jesus Name!
Amen!

10 PURPOSE

There is no doubt about it, you are God's daughter,

and he has a great purpose for your life. If there weren't a

purpose for your life, you wouldn't be here reading this book.

Allow this chapter to reaffirm that you are not here by

accident. God created you with something special in mind.

Your purpose will take you to new heights and give you even

more reason to live and to keep pushing. I often hear people

asking the question, what is my purpose in life? This is a

question that you must ask God during your prayer time, and

he will reveal it to you. The bible says, "And whatever you ask in prayer, you will receive if you have faith." Ask God to show you your purpose and ask him to show you how to operate in your purpose. It isn't enough to know what you are here for; you must also be sure that God gets the glory out of your purpose.

When you begin walking in purpose, you will also start to walk in freedom. Your purpose solidifies why God created you. You don't have to worry about approval and acceptance because when God gives you his stamp of approval, it trumps all others. When I think about walking in purpose, I think about catching a flight. Before you get on a plane, you pack your bag, making sure that you bring everything along that you need. You also make sure that you follow the guidelines of the airlines to prevent any issues at the time of taking your flight. The same is valid for living out your purpose. You pack a bag of only the essential items. You get rid of all of the things that could potentially weigh you down. You also consult with God about what he requires from you so that you can ascend in your purpose.

In my luggage, I have packed: boldness, fearlessness, faith, perseverance, and clothes to dress daily for the battle. I know that I need each of these things in my luggage to get on the flight of purpose. The job of the enemy is to come and attack our purpose. He wants to stop us from fulfilling our purpose. The enemy's position is to destroy the anointing and keep God's word from manifesting in our lives. I have news for the enemy; IT WILL NOT WORK.

I don't want to return to the old me. I've done too much work to resort to my old ways. I've cried too many tears to go back to the place of darkness. I've seen God do too many things in my life, not trust him to do even more. So, there's no need for a round-trip plane ticket.

Some people have flying anxiety. Walking in your purpose can be frightening. It makes you nervous because walking in purpose means you have surrendered all. The same happens when we get on our flight. We don't have control over the takeoff or landing. We have to trust that we will make it to our destination safely. Sometimes there is turbulence when you are up in the air, but you must trust that the pilot will safely get you to your destination. We must also trust God fully. During the turbulent times in the process, we must continue to have faith that we will fulfill our destiny.

As a woman, there are certain areas of our lives where we want to gain full access and control how things work out. We like to plan out our days to ensure that we meet every deadline and tackle every assignment, especially if it relates to our family. Sis, I'm sorry to tell you that you're not always going to know what is coming next. You are going to have to trust God without an itinerary. Don't be distracted by parts of the process that you don't know or understand. Distractions prevent us from giving full attention to something else. The enemy plan is to distract you from seeing and walking after your purpose. You must stay focused on your vision. You can't allow everything to frustrate you when you are walking in purpose. Some things no longer matter.

Ultimately the old tricks of the enemy can no longer make you feel defeated or "distract" you. Do you have faith that distraction is a battle you can claim in victory? "I did this so that your faith might not depend on the wisdom of the people, but on the power of God." -1 Corinthians 2:5 God is saying here several things about our thoughts vs. his power. When writing this, apostle Paul chose not to impress the people with his knowledge or skill with words. Instead, he presented the truth about Jesus as clearly as he could. God accompanied Paul's teaching with the demonstration of His power and His spirit. He wanted to fulfill his purpose and do it without the thought of people to decrease "distraction."

Living out purpose may look different from how people have seen you in the past. Living out purpose means you may walk alone and on a different course than others. The destination of purpose shifts your prayer towards trusting God and following his will.

Trusting God's plan for my life began when I realized that the plan is not mine, nor is the plan about me. "For I know the plans I have for you, declares the Lord, plans to prosper you and not to harm you, plans to give you hope and a future." ~Jeremiah 29:11. My favorite scripture states that God has a plan, and in his plan, we must prosper. This very message explains that there's hope and a future that lies during the journey of purpose.

May this book bless you to find rest in God. Find power in prayer. Become stronger in your walk. Remind you that you are the daughter of the most High God. You are God's Daughter! ~Tameria Weaver

SCRIPTURES

1. But you are a chosen people, a royal priesthood, a holy nation a people for God's own possession, to proclaim the virtues of Him who called you out of darkness into His marvelous light. (1 Peter 2:9)

2. Great are your purposes and might are your deeds. Your eyes are open to the ways of all mankind; you reward each person according to their conduct and as their deeds deserve. (Jeremiah 32:19)

3. I know that you can do all things; no purpose of yours can be thwarted. (Job 42:2)

4. For we are God's handiwork. Created in Christ Jesus to do good works, which God prepared in advance for us to do. (Ephesians 2:10)

PRAYER OF PURPOSE

Dear God,

God, this is your daughter here at your feet.

Thank you for my life. Thank you for my purpose. Thank you for preparing me for where you are taking me. Thank you for trusting me with this assignment.

I trust you with the next steps for my life. I know that you will take care of me throughout this journey.

Would you please continue to direct me and show me your way. God, please give me the strength to do your will when I don't know all the details. Please increase my faith so that I may please you.

God, my life is in your hands.

In Jesus Name.
Amen.

Made in the USA
Columbia, SC
27 August 2022

65433096R00067